FLOOD 2011

A PHOTO DOCUMENTARY OF THE RECORD FLOODING ACROSS CENTRAL NEW YORK

PRESENTED BY

PRESS & SUN-BULLETIN   STAR-GAZETTE   The Ithaca JOURNAL

ACKNOWLEDGMENTS

This book represents the strong work of the newsroom staffs of the Binghamton Press & Sun-Bulletin, the Star-Gazette of Elmira and The Ithaca Journal, assisted by colleagues from Gannett newspapers in Rochester and Westchester County. The team of photographers and reporters who captured these images included George Basler, Nancy Dooling, Ray Finger, Seth Harrison, Kevin Hogan, Jennifer Kingsley, Laurie Miner, William Moyer, My-Ly Nguyen, Steve Reilly, Jeff Richards, Brian Sharp, Casey Staff, Debbie Swartz, Michelle Terry, Simon Wheeler, Jason Whong and Tina Yee. This book also includes photographs contributed by our readers and freelance photographers. The book's narrative and final shape was the work of editors John Catlett, Mary Haupt, Frank Roessner and Al Vieira.

Published by Pediment Publishing, a division of The Pediment Group, Inc. www.pediment.com Printed in Canada.

FOREWORD

We knew foul weather was coming, but few saw history on the radar.

Remnants of Tropical Storm Lee were expected to pass over the Binghamton-Elmira-Ithaca area, and the forecast for Wednesday included a flood watch and the possibility of 3 inches of rain in Broome County, which had just been soaked by Tropical Storm Irene.

Lee didn't carry the fanfare that accompanied Irene's assault on the East Coast, but it carried massive amounts of water in its corpulent clouds: it dropped an estimated 45 trillion gallons across the United States. And when Lee parked above the Susquehanna River on Sept. 7, it unleashed torrential, unceasing rain for hours.

The region's residents witnessing the deluge, and knowing what it would do to an already saturated landscape, shared a common thought: Not again.

But this wasn't a repeat of the Flood of 2006. It was worse.

As the rain pounded the region and floodwaters rose, an estimated 20,000 people were evacuated in Broome County; thousands more from Tioga County to Elmira — more than 100,000 across the Northeast. Lives and property untouched in 2006 were immersed as the rivers swelled to record levels, streams surged from their banks and scoured fields and streets, and overwrought storm sewers backed up into houses and buildings. People fortunate enough to be living beyond the water's reach still found themselves cut off on all sides by submerged and washed-out roads and bridges.

In the Village of Owego, streets became canals and 90 percent of buildings downtown had water damage. Emergency shelters across the region filled as rapidly as the basements. Emergency personnel worked heroically and tirelessly, even as some of their own homes and cars were being enveloped.

Slowly the waters receded, and in their wake came a flood of compassion. It flowed from across the state and the nation, in the form of firefighters and emergency crews, arriving in National Guard helicopters and Red Cross vehicles. It came bearing blankets, medicine, fresh water, cleaning supplies — and encouragement.

Stricken by nature, we were blessed in equal measure by benevolence. These wonderful people — including many high school and college students — offered much more than helping hands. They provided comfort, smiles, and a reassuring presence.

The damage was severe, and for some people it was simply too much. They will seek a future elsewhere. But most flood victims are rebuilding their lives and homes, mourning the loss of mementos and heirlooms but clinging to the good memories and intending to add to that collection.

And they are finding scores of good-hearted people willing to help them. It's what people do in response to natural disaster. It is in such dire circumstances that we truly define ourselves as a community.

The job is enormous, and full recovery might take years. But the work is well begun, and with each restored basement, each replaced chair, each reclaimed home, the community is renewing itself. ■

TABLE OF CONTENTS

CHAPTER ONE

DAY ONE

By midday Wednesday, Sept. 7, manhole covers along Harry L Drive in Johnson City resembled lids on boiling tea kettles, frothing at the rims with water gushing up from the storm sewers. Across the region, firefighters and road crews were erecting barricades as streets flooded and creeks and streams swept across bridges.

Rain gauges were busy measuring the deluge. Lee was delivering three months' worth of rain in the span of a day — 3.6 inches in Ithaca over the course of the storm; 3.7 inches at Elmira Corning Regional Airport; 6 inches in Waverly; 8.4 inches in Owego; 8.9 inches at Greater Binghamton Airport; 10.4 inches in Apalachin.

Brett Chellis, Broome County's director of emergency services, said, "We have to be prepared for the worst. People need to be ready to move."

Shelters were opened across the region, the largest one at Binghamton University's Events Center.

Thousands of residents already were under mandatory evacuation, notified by reverse 911 calls and by firefighters going door-to-door. States of emergency were declared across several counties, and when Broome County announced no businesses were to be open Thursday, that triggered a rush to stores by those people who could get to them.

Many residents, especially those who had experienced the Flood of 2006, did not have to be told to leave home. They knew what all that rain meant. They packed what they could carry, moved as many of their belongings as possible to the top floor or crammed them into the highest cupboards, turned off the power and pilot lights, and left for higher ground.

Late Wednesday, the rain finally eased, but the water continued to cascade down the hillsides and the rivers continued to rise — as did the crest estimates. Throughout the night and into Thursday morning, people who had gone to bed feeling safe were awakened by police or emergency personnel and told to leave.

The storm's property damage toll was rising. ∎

OPPOSITE: Floodwaters inundated roads around the region the day Tropical Storm Lee struck.

JEFF RICHARDS / STAFF PHOTO

RIGHT: Sept. 7 was the first day of school for many districts in the region. By late morning, though, many schools were preparing to close early. Here, Alex Robinson Jr., 10, heads to Broadway Elementary School in Southport as Ray Hayes guards the crosswalk. JEFF RICHARDS / STAFF PHOTO

BELOW: A school bus eases its way through standing water on Route 38 in Newark Valley. LAURIE MINER / STAFF PHOTO

ABOVE: Standing water made driving risky on many streets, including College Avenue in Elmira. JEFF RICHARDS / STAFF PHOTO

ABOVE & LEFT: Debris collected in this stream parallel to Route 11 near the Main Street underpass in Kirkwood.

MICHELLE TERRY / STAFF PHOTOS

FAR LEFT: Heavy rains caused a creek to overflow and forced the closing of this stretch of Route 11 in Kirkwood.

MICHELLE TERRY / STAFF PHOTO

ABOVE: Local municipalities had to respond quickly as floodwaters covered streets and highways. Johnson City Fire Marshal Dave Nugent called for barricades to be put up on Leigh Street as water rushed down a hill and across the pavement. WILLIAM MOYER / STAFF PHOTO

RIGHT: Fallen trees, such as these behind the Mark Twain Golf Course in Horseheads, kept highway workers busy throughout the day. JEFF RICHARDS / STAFF PHOTO

ABOVE: Businesses, such as this one on North Street in Endicott, were quickly surrounded by rising water as heavy rains overwhelmed storm sewers. WILLIAM MOYER / STAFF PHOTO

LEFT: Many buildings, such as the CVS Pharmacy on Route 26 in West Corners near Endicott, became islands surrounded by floodwaters. WILLIAM MOYER / STAFF PHOTO

BOTTOM LEFT: The playground at Kirby Park in Nichols. JEFF RICHARDS / STAFF PHOTO

BELOW: This tent was set up for Nichols Old Home Day in Kirby Park. JEFF RICHARDS / STAFF PHOTO

ABOVE: Vehicles throughout the region quickly became submerged in floodwater. This pickup truck was trapped by an out-of-control Wappasening Creek along Route 282 near Nichols. JEFF RICHARDS / STAFF PHOTO

RIGHT: Debris caused many already swollen creeks to spill over their banks. JEFF RICHARDS / STAFF PHOTO

ABOVE: Fast-rising water caught many by surprise. It also spurred many people to help others in distress. Daniel Witney of Endicott carried Pat Crosby, alongside her husband, Chris Crosby, through a flooded intersection in West Corners near Endicott. The Crosbys were trying to get to dry ground when Witney, who had stopped at a nearby gas station, began helping evacuees cross the road. CASEY STAFF / STAFF PHOTO

ABOVE: Patty Desmond was among those shaken by the rapidly rising water on Route 26 in West Corners. Desmond was not immediately able to locate her children and had to wait for emergency workers to rescue her dogs.
CASEY STAFF / STAFF PHOTO

ABOVE: People helped each other cross the knee-high waters flooding Route 26. Many evacuees waited at the nearby Mobil gas station for their friends and relatives to be rescued by emergency personnel. CASEY STAFF / STAFF PHOTO

LEFT: Kathleen Rotunna, of West Corners, is no stranger to floods: She was a victim of the 2006 flood as well. This time, she and her dog, Nala, made it safely across Route 26 to the Mobil station. But she had to leave her cats behind when she fled her home. CASEY STAFF / STAFF PHOTO

TOP & BOTTOM: Emergency personnel respond to the flooding in West Corners, near Endicott. Many residents there were forced to evacuate. CASEY STAFF / STAFF PHOTOS

ABOVE: West Corners flooded when water from Nanticoke Creek poured over a floodwall. CASEY STAFF / STAFF PHOTO

LEFT: In Binghamton, the rain-swollen Susquehanna River approached the deck of the South Washington Street Bridge. NANCY DOOLING / STAFF PHOTO

ABOVE: Main Street in Kirkwood was among the many roads closed Wednesday. This photo was taken from Route 11. NANCY DOOLING / STAFF PHOTO

TOP RIGHT: Water Street in Newark Valley lived up to its name. LAURIE MINER / STAFF PHOTO

RIGHT: A mudslide shut down Interstate 88 in the Town of Fenton. Mud and trees slid down the mountain onto the highway between Port Crane and Chenango Bridge.

CONTRIBUTED PHOTO

ABOVE: Workers with the New York State Department of Environmental Conservation in Kirkwood tighten bolts that secured the floodwalls placed on the South Washington Street Bridge in Binghamton. CASEY STAFF / STAFF PHOTO

CHAPTER TWO
DAY TWO

Thursday called for patience and prayers as the region waited for the rivers to crest.

The emergency shelter at Binghamton University, with a capacity of around 1,600, was full by that afternoon.

One of the refugees was Dennis Brink of Kirkwood, who had been evacuated from Conklin five years earlier. "The first time around, I lost everything," he said. "This time around, there's not much to lose."

At Lourdes Hospital on Riverside Drive in Binghamton, a flood wall had been erected after the 2006 flood caused an evacuation of the facility and extensive damage to the ground floor. This time the Susquehanna River crested even higher — at 25.71 feet — but the wall held.

In other places, however, the river easily overcame barriers. Once behind those walls, the water had no natural outlet, so it quickly engulfed more neighborhoods.

In Athens, Pa., nestled between the Susquehanna and Chemung rivers, the water level reached 10 feet on Center Street. More than half of the borough's streets were severely damaged. Further downstream, other Pennsylvania communities clear to Harrisburg were ravaged as well.

President Obama declared a federal emergency in 15 New York counties and 42 more in Pennsylvania. New York Gov. Andrew Cuomo arrived to survey the damage by helicopter. Other sightseeing was discouraged, however, due to the lingering danger. In Binghamton, National Guard troops joined police and city workers in turning away gawkers at the entrances to downtown.

It's understandable to be fascinated by such a display of nature's might, but there were thousands of lives being damaged. The full scope of that nightmare was revealed in the next 48 hours. ∎

OPPOSITE: Floodwater covered West Corners near Linnaeus W. West Elementary School, lower right, in the Town of Union. The intersection of Day Hollow Road and Route 26 can be seen at top right. SIMON WHEELER / STAFF PHOTO

ABOVE: Water gushed from the floodwall near the entrance to the South Washington Street Bridge from North Shore Drive in Binghamton. CASEY STAFF / STAFF PHOTO

ABOVE: Water flowed just inches below Memorial Bridge on Riverside Drive in Binghamton. CASEY STAFF / STAFF PHOTO

RIGHT: Six Mile Creek in Ithaca receded a bit from its highest water level just downstream from the Plain Street Bridge. SIMON WHEELER / STAFF PHOTO

ABOVE: Ithaca's assistant superintendent of public works, Ray Benjamin, checked on South Albany Street as a car inched its way through the floodwater. SIMON WHEELER / STAFF PHOTO

ABOVE: Traffic along Route 13A in Ithaca had to be diverted to Route 79, causing long delays. Here, an Ithaca Police officer was checking the depth of the water on Meadow Street. SIMON WHEELER / STAFF PHOTO

LEFT: A man inspected floodwaters outside Titus Towers II senior housing in Ithaca. SIMON WHEELER / STAFF PHOTO

BELOW: Ithaca Police pushed this disabled car out of floodwaters on Meadow Street. SIMON WHEELER / STAFF PHOTO

ABOVE & RIGHT: Water inundated Scott Brown's garage on Wood Street in Ithaca, giving 14-year-old C.J. White the idea to go fishing off Brown's porch.

SIMON WHEELER / STAFF PHOTOS

ABOVE: From left, Ithaca Housing Authority maintenance worker Jeff Little showed Titus Towers residents Carol Fry, Domenico Ciotti and another resident pictures of the water inside Ciotti's car before he moved it out of the deepest water in the Titus Towers parking lot. SIMON WHEELER / STAFF PHOTO

ABOVE: Choconut Creek receded under this bridge on Juneberry Road in Vestal, but a day later the water was over the bridge and up the sides of the banks. KEVIN HOGAN / STAFF PHOTO

LEFT: This bridge over Choconut Creek on Meeker Road in Vestal collapsed. KEVIN HOGAN / STAFF PHOTO

OPPOSITE: Ithaca Falls, as seen from the Lake Street Bridge. SIMON WHEELER / STAFF PHOTO

RIGHT: Floodwater rose above the surface of this bridge on Front Street in Vestal. CASEY STAFF / STAFF PHOTO

BELOW: Workers had to clean up debris after a dike failed along Bentley Creek and water spilled onto Front Street in Wellsburg. JEFF RICHARDS / STAFF PHOTO

ABOVE: A backhoe was brought in to repair a dike along Bentley Creek that gave way, flooding Front Street in Wellsburg. JEFF RICHARDS / STAFF PHOTO

ABOVE: Floodwaters dumped debris along Lockwood Run in the Town of Chemung. CONTRIBUTED PHOTO

LEFT: Water rushed along the newly constructed Laurel Hill Road outside Milan. JENNIFER KINGSLEY / STAFF PHOTO

OPPOSITE: Downtown Owego was inundated after the Susquehanna River, top left, overflowed its banks. The Tioga County Courthouse can be seen at top right.

SIMON WHEELER / STAFF PHOTO

ABOVE: Two Johnson City residents paddled their canoe – their pets in tow – through the intersection of North Broad and Brown streets. JOE GERONIMO / CONTRIBUTED PHOTO

RIGHT: Homes and vehicles were inundated when Olive Street in Johnson City was flooded. JOE GERONIMO / CONTRIBUTED PHOTO

TOP: Gov. Andrew M. Cuomo held a press conference in the Broome County Sheriff's Office to reinforce the need for people to evacuate their homes when called upon to do so. CASEY STAFF / STAFF PHOTO

BOTTOM: This tractor-trailer made its way through water that covered parts of Route 220 between Milan and North Towanda, Pa. The truck's cargo: a boat. GARTH WADE / CONTRIBUTED PHOTO

OPPOSITE: Evacuees crowded the Binghamton University Events Center Thursday. GEORGE BASLER / STAFF PHOTO

ABOVE: A raging Six Mile Creek ate away at Banks Road in the Town of Caroline near the newly built bridge over Six Mile Creek. Members of the Caroline Town Highway Department installed concrete barriers to keep motor vehicles away. DAVE BURBANK / CONTRIBUTED PHOTO

ABOVE: Tom Young, near his garage on German Cross Road in Ithaca. Portions of the Six Mile Creek bed eroded upstream from his house, causing his entire backyard to flood. DAVE BURBANK / CONTRIBUTED PHOTO

RIGHT: Brooktondale volunteer firefighter Brandon Cary set up a portable pump to help remove water from the basement of a house on Valley Road in Brooktondale.

DAVE BURBANK / CONTRIBUTED PHOTO

ABOVE: Floodwaters from a tributary of Cayuta Creek washed out the base support for a railroad track that parallels state Route 34 south of Lockwood. JEFF RICHARDS / STAFF PHOTO

ABOVE: Brenno Varanda, foreground, and Jonathan Brownell of Murray Street in Binghamton helped Brownell's landlady, also of Murray Street, by bailing out the basement. TINA YEE / STAFF PHOTO

LEFT: A closed road didn't stop this motorcyclist from crossing Kelly Road near East Smithfield. A day earlier, the road was covered with floodwater. JENNIFER KINGSLEY / STAFF PHOTO

BELOW: DeShawn Harrell, 14, of Binghamton, watched the Chenango River spill over the top of a floodwall. Police later ordered people to move two blocks west of Front Street. TINA YEE / STAFF PHOTO

ABOVE: Binghamton police used a loudspeaker to order people to move away from Front Street as the Chenango River began breaching the floodwall. TINA YEE / STAFF PHOTO

ABOVE: Sara Kenn of Binghamton headed to her sister's place after she heard that Front Street was being evacuated in case of a levy breach. TINA YEE / STAFF PHOTO

TOP LEFT: National Guard joined several police agencies in keeping people away from the Chenango River levy.
TINA YEE / STAFF PHOTO

LEFT: Furniture was piled up on the porch of a home on Front Street near Riverside Drive as water from the Susquehanna and Chenango rivers crept closer.
TINA YEE / STAFF PHOTO

ABOVE: Endicott police officer Dale Cioci stood watch on the bridge that connects Endicott to Vestal. The bridge was closed after the Susquehanna River rose to within a foot of the bridge deck. WILLIAM MOYER / STAFF PHOTO

RIGHT: A house on Marshland Road east of the Village of Owego burned as high water from the Susquehanna River delayed firefighters. SIMON WHEELER / STAFF PHOTO

OPPOSITE: The Village of Candor, looking south from Route 96B. The Citgo gas station is at lower left.
SIMON WHEELER / STAFF PHOTO

CHAPTER THREE

DAY THREE

THE REGION AWOKE TO A vast, brown swamp stretching from Chenango County to Chemung County in New York and from Susquehanna County to Bradford County in Pennsylvania. The main highways between Broome and Tioga counties — Route 17/I-86, Route 17C and Route 434 — all were closed, and would remain so for days.

Many rural roads across those counties were also closed — some due to standing water; others because they had been undercut by the rushing water. Travel in all directions was detoured.

As the waters slowly receded, they revealed a thick layer of mud — sickeningly accompanied by sewage in many places. Gray high-water marks stained shrubs, trees, and buildings. But as much as people wanted to return home and begin the process of disposal and recovery, they had to wait for inspectors to determine if structures were safe.

Some 2,000 buildings in Binghamton were damaged, according to city officials. Owego Mayor Ed Arrington said 90 percent of the buildings in downtown Owego had taken on water. Every community had to take stock.

In Johnson City, employees of the PETCO store on Harry L. Drive were allowed back into the building, only to find a heartbreaking scene. More than 100 animals had perished in the flood. While the employees were able to save more than 100 animals and transport them to other stores, the loss triggered widespread outrage among people who wondered how it could happen.

Remarkably, only one human life was known to be lost to the flood: 95-year-old Dorothy Guethe was found dead of hypothermia in her home in Wysox, Pa. ■

OPPOSITE: This car was abandoned on Laurelton Drive in West Corners, near Endicott. CASEY STAFF / STAFF PHOTO

RIGHT: The intersection of Vestal Avenue and South Washington Street was adorned with caution tape and roadblocks as Broome County remained under a state of emergency. CASEY STAFF / STAFF PHOTO

OPPOSITE: With no other way of getting around the Town of Conklin, some residents used the railroad tracks. MICHELLE TERRY / STAFF PHOTO

BELOW: This house along the Susquehanna River in Ulster gets flooded every few years. This year, though, the water was especially deep. JENNIFER KINGSLEY / STAFF PHOTO

TOP: With school canceled because of the flood, Gabriel Honnick, left, and Hunter Baker rode their bikes through the parking lot of the Coin Laundry on Carl Street in West Corners. Honnick's family was evacuated from their apartment on Oxford Street. Baker's father owns Response Audio, next to the Coin Laundry. CASEY STAFF / STAFF PHOTO

BOTTOM: Nanticoke Creek flooded Hamilton's Doll-Up Center, an auto detail shop on Carl Street in West Corners. CASEY STAFF / STAFF PHOTO

OPPOSITE: Debris collected on the opposite side of the floodwall at the end of Carl Street in West Corners. CASEY STAFF / STAFF PHOTO

ABOVE: Floodwater covered the ball fields along Thomas Avenue in Sayre, Pa. JENNIFER KINGSLEY / STAFF PHOTO

RIGHT: Richard Love was one of the West Corners Fire Department volunteer firefighters who distributed water during a boil-water advisory. CASEY STAFF / STAFF PHOTO

FAR RIGHT: Flooding forced the closing of Sheshequin Road between Ulster and Athens, Pa.

JENNIFER KINGSLEY / STAFF PHOTO

ABOVE: Floodwaters washed this doghouse into Bridge Street in the Town of Kirkwood. MICHELLE TERRY / STAFF PHOTO

ABOVE: Floodwaters washed this doghouse onto Bridge Street in the Town of Kirkwood. MICHELLE TERRY / STAFF PHOTO

LEFT: Curious onlookers took in the damage along South Main Street in Athens. JENNIFER KINGSLEY / STAFF PHOTO

OPPOSITE: Part of the shoulder along Route 96 near the intersection with Route 38 in Owego was damaged all the way to the white line. SIMON WHEELER / STAFF PHOTO

LEFT: Emergency crews checked for occupants and posted notices on the windows of flooded houses on Powers Road in Conklin. MICHELLE TERRY / STAFF PHOTO

BOTTOM LEFT: As the Chenango River receded, dead fish could be found stuck in the mud along a walkway in downtown Binghamton. TINA YEE / STAFF PHOTO

OPPOSITE: Emergency crews checked flooded houses on Powers Road in Conklin. MICHELLE TERRY / STAFF PHOTO

BELOW: Tyler Kisacky, left, and Tyler Gunn, both of Brown Street in Johnson City, delivered a pump to Gunn's home the only way they could. TINA YEE / STAFF PHOTO

ABOVE: Many riverside buildings in downtown Binghamton, such as The Galleria, had to pump water out of their lower levels. TINA YEE / STAFF PHOTO

RIGHT: Peter Pappas of Binghamton helped his sister pump water out of her house on Avon Road.

TINA YEE / STAFF PHOTO

OPPOSITE: Brian Kasmarcik of Chenango Bridge had to search for a storm drain along Pratt Avenue in Johnson City as he pumped water out of a rental property his father owns. TINA YEE / STAFF PHOTO

ABOVE: Christine Shanovskiy of Chenango Bridge and her boyfriend, Dan Marvin, of Chenango Forks photographed the Chenango River in downtown Binghamton as the river receded.

TINA YEE / STAFF PHOTO

LEFT: North Street in Owego, looking south.

BELOW: A waterline on a wall near the Court Street Bridge in Binghamton showed how high the Chenango River had risen.

RIGHT: As floodwaters receded, Lake and Main streets in downtown Owego were left with a coating of mud.

BRIAN SHARP / STAFF PHOTO

BELOW: Front Street in Wellsburg was closed to traffic from Main Street to Berwick Turnpike for cleanup after floodwaters receded. Equipment came from all over, including the City of Elmira, Chemung County and the towns of Ashland and Southport. RAY FINGER / STAFF PHOTO

ABOVE: A City of Elmira water truck cleaned mud off Front Street in Wellsburg.

RAY FINGER / STAFF PHOTO

ABOVE: Mud had to be cleared from the front of the Wellsburg Diner. RAY FINGER / STAFF PHOTO

LEFT: Inside the Wellsburg Diner, floodwaters rose to between 4 and 5 feet deep, leaving behind a layer of "flood mud." RAY FINGER / STAFF PHOTO

ABOVE: Emergency personnel had to navigate South Main Street in Athens, Pa., as they transported flood victims back to their homes to pick up medical supplies.

JEFF RICHARDS / STAFF PHOTO

LEFT: This car was almost submerged on Maple Street in Athens, Pa. JEFF RICHARDS / STAFF PHOTO

FAR LEFT: Owego residents congregated near the standing water on the south end of Main Street.

SIMON WHEELER / STAFF PHOTO

RIGHT: Kyle Slavetskas, with the Owego Fire Department, distributed bottled water to residents on Front Street in Owego. BRIAN SHARP / STAFF PHOTO

BELOW: Former chef Scott Smith of Owego cooked for his fellow evacuees at the American Red Cross shelter at the Abide in the Vine Center near Lockheed Martin in Owego. Smith was the only person cooking food for a group of people that fluctuated between 175 and 300.

SIMON WHEELER / STAFF PHOTO

OPPOSITE: Karl Tiemann, 82, of Delphine Street in Owego was evacuated by boat along with his wife, Theresa, after signaling a helicopter with a light from his porch. The Tiemanns then stayed at a shelter being run by the Tompkins County Chapter of the American Red Cross.

SIMON WHEELER / STAFF PHOTO

CHAPTER FOUR

THE AFTERMATH

Broome County Executive Patrick Brennan said it would take years to recover from the flood, and his is the voice of experience: just six months earlier, Broome County had received its last payment from the Federal Emergency Management Agency for damage from the June 2006 flood.

FEMA arrived this time with 10,000 liters of water, 80,000 meals, thousands of cots and blankets. It also dispatched teams to assess properties.

Power was quickly restored in most areas, but pockets across the region would have to wait a few days. The widespread boil-water orders also lingered until municipal officials could determine if the supply was safe.

Evacuees started returning to their homes on the weekend — some would have to wait until the following week — and within minutes, the trash mountains began forming on curbs. Aided by relatives, friends and neighbors, people began the task of discarding ruined furniture, carpeting, draperies, clothing — anything and everything that had been soaked.

Many rooms were stripped down to the studs — and those were closely inspected for moisture or mold. Basements were pumped out, often by friendly firefighters from far away. These included some from New York City, who skipped the 10th anniversary 9/11 memorial service to help out upstate because upstate people had rushed to help them in the aftermath of that horrific day.

For the fortunate, restoration required only a dried basement, some new paneling and perhaps a new water heater or other appliance. But in the neighborhoods where those trash mountains rose, there was more work to be done — and accomplished quickly — with winter on its way.

The damage assessments also will take time, even as repairs are under way. Less than two weeks after the flood, New York Assemblyman Gary Finch, of Union Springs, estimated $100 million in Tioga County alone — including $44 million in Owego. Stretch that across the bi-state region and the final toll will be staggering. ∎

OPPOSITE: Flood marks were apparent on this red maple tree on Third Avenue in the Twin Orchards neighborhood of Vestal. DEBBIE SWARTZ / STAFF PHOTO

ABOVE: Heavy flood damage in West Corners kept residents away for several days. STEVE REILLY / STAFF PHOTO

RIGHT: A two-family home on Front Street in Binghamton was condemned until the electrical and gas panels could be inspected and repaired. Meanwhile, tenants had to remain in shelters. CASEY STAFF / STAFF PHOTO

FAR RIGHT: Selena Galadriel and her mother, who live on Theron Street in Johnson City, said they were prepared for the recent flood after experiencing the flood of 2006.
CASEY STAFF / STAFF PHOTO

ABOVE: Damaged belongings quickly piled up in Johnson City. STEVE REILLY / STAFF PHOTO

LEFT: Xeque Wales surveyed the debris piled in front of her home on North Hudson Street in Johnson City. STEVE REILLY / STAFF PHOTO

OPPOSITE: Flood-damaged items from the Ligas family's home lined the curb on Concord Street in Johnson City. STEVE REILLY / STAFF PHOTO

RIGHT: Johnson City firefighters battled a blaze on Crocker Avenue while the flood-damaged village water supply was operating off a single well. STEVE REILLY / STAFF PHOTO

OPPOSITE: The foundation of George Elmy's home on Harvard Street in West Corners was destroyed. STEVE REILLY / STAFF PHOTO

BELOW: Trucks were stranded in the water off Route 17 in Johnson City. DEBBIE SWARTZ / STAFF PHOTO

LEFT: Volunteers served food prepared by Sodexo workers at Binghamton University's Events Center. Those staying at the shelter received three meals a day, plus snacks. Pawel Nowacki, retail director for Sodexo, said special diets were followed for those with food allergies. DEBBIE SWARTZ / STAFF PHOTO

OPPOSITE: It took days for water to recede from much of Front Street in Vestal. DEBBIE SWARTZ / STAFF PHOTO

BELOW: Residents of Meadow Street in Binghamton's First Ward assessed the damage. DEBBIE SWARTZ / STAFF PHOTO

ABOVE: This Binghamton home suffered interior damage.

MICHAEL FORSTER ROTHBART / CONTRIBUTED PHOTO

RIGHT: All kinds of debris littered sidewalks on Washington Street in Binghamton as businesses and homeowners cleaned up the mess left by the flood.

DEBBIE SWARTZ / STAFF PHOTO

FAR RIGHT: Competition Kitchen and Baths on South Washington Street in Binghamton suffered heavy damage.

DEBBIE SWARTZ / STAFF PHOTO

THIS PAGE & OPPOSITE: MacArthur Elementary School, on Vestal Avenue in Binghamton, was extensively damaged and might have to be rebuilt. The Binghamton City School District was evaluating its options.

GEORGE BASLER / STAFF PHOTOS

ABOVE: Mud left by receding floodwaters only complicated the cleanup in the Owego area.

BRIAN SHARP / STAFF PHOTO

OPPOSITE: As the removal of damaged items from his home continued, James Hoover, 23, of Apalachin took a short break.

BRIAN SHARP / STAFF PHOTO

RIGHT: People salvaged what they could from their Binghamton-area homes once they were permitted to return to them. MICHAEL FORSTER ROTHBART / CONTRIBUTED PHOTO

FAR RIGHT: Flooded cars were abandoned in Johnson City. MICHAEL FORSTER ROTHBART / CONTRIBUTED PHOTO

BELOW: Twin Orchards residents left their flooded Vestal neighborhood with bags of belongings after being allowed into the area for the first time since it was flooded. DEBBIE SWARTZ / STAFF PHOTO

ABOVE: The inside of PETCO in Johnson City, seen through the front door, was littered with damaged merchandise. MY-LY NGUYEN / STAFF PHOTO

RIGHT: A Johnson City resident surveyed some of the flooded streets and businesses in the village. MICHAEL FORSTER ROTHBART / CONTRIBUTED PHOTO

ABOVE: Cleanup of flood damage in Athens, Pa., was clearly going to take awhile. JEFF RICHARDS / STAFF PHOTO

LEFT: Floodwaters began to recede on Bradley Avenue in Conklin. NANCY DOOLING / STAFF PHOTO

ABOVE: Cars remained partially submerged at a lot next to North Avenue in the Village of Owego. In the background, mud stuck to leaves that were submerged during the flood.

JASON WHONG / STAFF PHOTO

LEFT: A wall of destroyed books surrounded Riverow Bookshop in the Village of Owego. JASON WHONG / STAFF PHOTO

BELOW: Refuse piled up in front of homes on East Front Street in Owego. DEBBIE SWARTZ / STAFF PHOTO

ABOVE: Robert and Amber O'Hara of Ormond Trailer Park in West Corners had purchased a large supply of groceries shortly before the flood, only to lose it all.
CASEY STAFF / STAFF PHOTO

ABOVE: Scott Mitchell and his girlfriend, Tammy O'Hara, inside their flood-damaged home in Ormond Trailer Park in West Corners. They lived in the park for 10 years, but moved into this trailer just five months earlier.
CASEY STAFF / STAFF PHOTO

RIGHT: Ken McRorie, an Ormond Trailer Park resident, said he lost everything he owns in the flood. He lived in the park for more than 15 years. CASEY STAFF / STAFF PHOTO

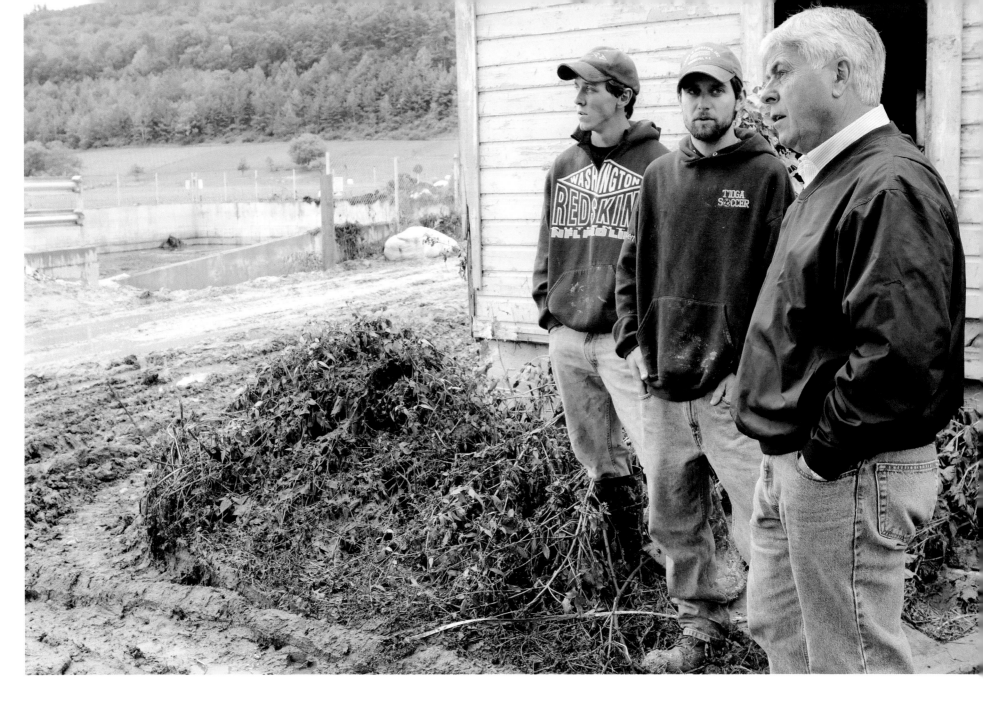

ABOVE: New York State Agriculture Commissioner Darrel J. Aubertine, right, listens to John Engelbert, left, and his brother Joe describe the devastation to Engelbert Farms in Nichols, which they own with their parents. JASON WHONG / STAFF PHOTO

TOP: Some of the damage at Elmira Grinding Works in Wellsburg. RAY FINGER / STAFF PHOTO

BOTTOM: The flood damaged the Whole in the Wall restaurant on Binghamton's South Side.

MY-LY NGUYEN / STAFF PHOTO

OPPOSITE: The hall in the basement of the Church of the Blessed Sacrament in Johnson City was heavily damaged when floodwater filled the room to the ceiling.

CASEY STAFF / STAFF PHOTO

ABOVE: Mud coated this playground in a park in the Village of Nichols. DEBBIE SWARTZ / STAFF PHOTO

OPPOSITE: This bridge on East River Road in the Village of Nichols was extensively damaged by mud and debris from the Susquehanna River. DEBBIE SWARTZ / STAFF PHOTO

RIGHT: Bailey Hollow Bridge in the Town of Maine was destroyed by the flood. Town officials said it will cost the town $5 million to $7 million to recover from the flood.
STEVE REILLY / STAFF PHOTO

OPPOSITE: Flooding wiped away a portion of Struble Road in the Town of Union, leaving a large gap near Struble Sports Facility. STEVE REILLY / STAFF PHOTO

BELOW: A large section of Pollard Hill Road in the Town of Maine was destroyed by the flood. STEVE REILLY / STAFF PHOTO

ABOVE: More damage to Pollard Hill Road in the Town of Maine.
STEVE REILLY / STAFF PHOTO

CHAPTER FIVE
CLEANUP AND RECOVERY

MICHELLE DECKER OF ATHENS, PA., spoke for legions of people when she said, "The hardest part was taking everything we had and putting it on the curb."

Thousands of families went through that ordeal, and thousands more helped haul out the trash and clean and refurnish houses. Appliances and furniture, clothes and cars — all can be replaced. Old photos and heirlooms and other treasured things cannot be — but life can continue without them.

And so it does. In some places, aside from the "silt skirt" adorning shrubs and trees at the high-water mark, things returned fairly quickly to almost-normal. But in other places, much more time will be required — and in a few there really isn't much recovery possible. Some homes have been abandoned; some will have to be razed. Perhaps new ones will rise one day.

The great flood left a staggering mess, but it's amazing what elbow grease can accomplish when so many elbows are used in concert. The flood caused a lot of tears, but it also produced lifetime bonds between good and generous people, many of whom were strangers before they were brought together by necessity. The recovery effort has buoyed the spirits of both victims and volunteers.

That forward-looking attitude is seen across the region today. In Binghamton, MacArthur Elementary School students and teachers have been relocated and class is in session. Businesses are getting back up to speed, too. And evacuees have returned to nursing homes and assisted-living facilities. Among these are Clinton Cash, who just turned 100, and said it was "great" to return to The Hearth at Castle Gardens after several weeks away.

He stayed with his daughter in Endwell after being displaced and counted himself lucky, but said, "I missed the camaraderie. We're family here."

It could be said we're all family here across the flooded region. We got through the crisis together, and we'll continue to restore our communities together. ∎

OPPOSITE: Mark Vosbury hauled piles of damaged items from the basement of his two rental properties on Conklin Avenue in Conklin. Vosbury's auto sales company, located adjacent to the two homes, was also damaged.

SETH HARRISON / STAFF PHOTO

TOP: Joe Rafferty, a glazer at Northeastern Plate Glass in Binghamton, was among the employees who helped remove water and clean up the building it shares with EDI. CASEY STAFF / STAFF PHOTO

BOTTOM: Luke Washington of Northeastern Plate Glass sprayed down some of the hundreds of curtain rods that were submerged in floodwater. CASEY STAFF / STAFF PHOTO

OPPOSITE: Johnson City Public Works Department employees worked long hours to clean up after the flood. Here, Roland Smith, left, Cody Smith, center, and Evan Varrastro remove trash from the curbs on Oakdale Road. CASEY STAFF / STAFF PHOTO

ABOVE: Sweepers cleaned up Washington Street near Binghamton University's Downtown Center. DEBBIE SWARTZ / STAFF PHOTO

LEFT: Workers removed debris from McKinney Real Estate's office at Route 434 and South Washington Street in Binghamton. DEBBIE SWARTZ / STAFF PHOTO

FAR LEFT: Debris collected along a fence near BAE Systems in Westover. DEBBIE SWARTZ / STAFF PHOTO

RIGHT: Rubber gloves and masks were the order of the day as the cleanup began. MICHAEL FORSTER ROTHBART / CONTRIBUTED PHOTO

OPPOSITE: Neighbors on Kirkwood's Main Street took a break from the cleanup effort and gathered for a picnic. From left are Catherine Schuldt, Lucy Glover, Jack Glover and Jerome Schuldt. NANCY DOOLING / STAFF PHOTO

BELOW: Friends, relatives and total strangers came together to haul flood-soaked furniture and debris to the curbs. MICHAEL FORSTER ROTHBART / CONTRIBUTED PHOTO

ABOVE: Karen McCann cries as she tells David Tanenhaus, director of the Binghamton Housing Authority, she can no longer afford to stay in a hotel. She was displaced when the flood damaged her apartment building in downtown Binghamton. "I just want to go home," McCann said. CASEY STAFF / STAFF PHOTO

RIGHT: Gander Mountain was flooded for a second time in five years. This time, the damage was too severe and the big-box outdoors retailer announced it would be closing its Johnson City location for good. CASEY STAFF / STAFF PHOTO

ABOVE: As cleanup began on the weekend, there was nowhere to haul the debris because the landfill was closed.

MICHAEL FORSTER ROTHBART / CONTRIBUTED

RIGHT: Good Samaritans in pickup trucks arrived at cleanup sites and distributed water and food.

MICHAEL FORSTER ROTHBART / CONTRIBUTED

FAR RIGHT: Charley Decker of Ridgebury helped his son Larry Decker clean out his house on Maple Street in Athens, Pa. JEFF RICHARDS / STAFF PHOTO

113

ABOVE: Larry Decker of Maple Street in Athens, Pa., and his wife, Michelle, found an old Utica Club beer can as they cleaned out their house. JEFF RICHARDS / STAFF PHOTO

LEFT: Damaged refrigerators such as this one on Maple Street in Athens, Pa., were a common sight after the flood. Jeff Guiles of Guiles Hauling and Recycling in Spencer hauled this one away. JEFF RICHARDS / STAFF PHOTO

BELOW: More damaged property remained along the streets of Athens, Pa. JEFF RICHARDS / STAFF PHOTO

TOP: One mud-covered street down, many more to go in Athens, Pa. JEFF RICHARDS / STAFF PHOTO

BOTTOM: A National Guard unit from Wellsboro helped control traffic on South Main Street in Athens, Pa.
JEFF RICHARDS / STAFF PHOTO

OPPOSITE: Dannette Dunfee and her daughter Wendy Bishop, both employees at Curves on South Keystone Avenue in Sayre, Pa., sorted clothing that was donated to the business for flood victims. JEFF RICHARDS / STAFF PHOTO

ABOVE: Dehumidifier systems removed moisture from BAE Systems in Westover. MY-LY NGUYEN / STAFF PHOTO

ABOVE: Tom Sheredy and P.J. Corry, with the help of retired and off-duty Johnson City firefighters and their families, organized a free lunch for flood victims in Westover. Here, Sheredy grills hamburgers near Endwell Street and Oakdale Road. CASEY STAFF / STAFF PHOTO

LEFT: Kirsten Fuller, left, and Karaleah Scelsia, members of the Twin Orchards Baptist Church youth group, helped clean up a flooded property on Valley Road in Vestal.

DEBBIE SWARTZ / STAFF PHOTO

ABOVE: Tyler Blazey, left, Stephen Blazey, center, and Steve Blazey cleaned out their cousin's house on Myrtle Street in Vestal. The homeowner, Mike Fisher, works for the Vestal Fire Department and was helping to evacuate flood victims while his house was filling with 13 feet of water. CASEY STAFF / STAFF PHOTO

LEFT: ASPCA member Christopher Hersha of Florida, left, helped fellow member Kelly Hickey of New Jersey examine a cat belonging to a displaced tenant of Woodburn Court Apartments in downtown Binghamton. Animals were exposed to high levels of carbon monoxide from equipment used to pump water from the building. CASEY STAFF / STAFF PHOTO

ABOVE: Destroyed merchandise from Toys 'R' Us on Harry L Drive in Johnson City wound up in a dumpster.
SETH HARRISON / STAFF PHOTO

LEFT: The vacant lot at the former Anitec site on Charles Street in Binghamton became a temporary storage site for debris bound for the Broome County landfill. Tony Fleming was one of the Public Works Department workers on the scene. SETH HARRISON / STAFF PHOTO

TOP: Jim Laskowski of Fox Construction helped remove destroyed merchandise from Party City on Harry L Drive in Johnson City. SETH HARRISON / STAFF PHOTO

BOTTOM: As crews from the Johnson City Department of Public Works cleaned up debris, Jennifer Kirkland and Jackie Blakeslee consoled each other in front of Blakeslee's home on North Street in Johnson City. With them was neighbor Jim Muska. SETH HARRISON / STAFF PHOTO

OPPOSITE: Tony Starks swept water and muck into a storm sewer in front of his home on North Street in Johnson City. SETH HARRISON / STAFF PHOTO

ABOVE: Giovanni Gambino of Stefano Paving & Excavating added the final touches to the newly paved sidewalk outside of the CVS Pharmacy in West Corners, near Endicott. Fast-flowing floodwaters had surrounded the store and damaged the sidewalk. CASEY STAFF / STAFF PHOTO

LEFT: McKenna Warren, 22, left, and Sabrina Chilson, 26, employees of Chemung Canal Trust Co., helped clean up co-worker Cortni Brunk's home on Front Street in Wellsburg. JASON WHONG / STAFF PHOTO

BELOW: Chesapeake Energy Corp., volunteers and local residents were offered free meals by Great Plains Oilfield Rentals as cleanup efforts continued in Athens, Pa. JENNIFER KINGSLEY / STAFF PHOTO

ABOVE: Flood victim Octavia Moffett of Elm Street in Binghamton is given a case of water from the Food Bank of the Southern Tier outside the Boys and Girls Club on Clinton Street. The Sunflower Park Committee, a neighborhood association, worked with the food bank to bring the donated goods to the area. SETH HARRISON / STAFF PHOTO

RIGHT: These "Wizard of Oz" dolls belonged to Tammy Porcari, 19, of Owego. Her mother, Cheri Porcari, said the dolls had become waterlogged and were probably not salvageable. SETH HARRISON / STAFF PHOTO

OPPOSITE: Joe Bellgraph, 24, left, and Hannah Scouten, 22, helped their neighbor, John Allen, at his house on Church Street in Wellsburg. JASON WHONG / STAFF PHOTO

ABOVE: Millie Montgomery, an employee at Jane's Diner in Conklin, places ceramic mugs on a table outside the restaurant. The restaurant was one of many along Conklin Ave. that was closed due to flood damage.

SETH HARRISON / STAFF PHOTO

LEFT: Ruined books and other media are piled in front of a house on Front Street in Owego. JASON WHONG / STAFF PHOTO

OPPOSITE: Marlene Steenburg, left, gets help cleaning her flooded home in Owego. Steenburg, the pastor at Memorial Baptist Church in Vestal, got assistance from members of her congregation, including Waneta Vallese, right, of Endicott. Steenburg's husband, Terry, is the pastor at First Baptist Church in Owego. Members of his congregation also helped with the cleanup.

SETH HARRISON / STAFF PHOTO

ABOVE: Bill Kane, of JRG Transport, disconnects a hose after draining his water tanker into the sewer on Valley Road in the Twin Orchards section of Vestal. SETH HARRISON / STAFF PHOTO

ABOVE: Tammy O'Hara and her boyfriend, Scott Mitchell, loaded up a truck with personal belongings recovered from their home in Ormond Trailer Park, West Corners. O'Hara and Mitchell have lived in the park for 10 years, but moved into this trailer just five months earlier. CASEY STAFF / STAFF PHOTO

RIGHT: Tom and Pam Donovan stand inside their gutted home on Talcott St. in Owego. With the help of teachers, staff, and the football team from Owego Free Academy, they were able to remove all the damaged sheetrock and flooring. Pam Donovan is the secretary to the principal at the high school. SETH HARRISON / STAFF PHOTO

ABOVE: Joe Engelbert, left, and his brother John, who own Engelbert Farms in Nichols with their parents, carried lumber to a barn so they could build a ramp for their farm equipment.

I Cleaned My House last week

Sorry You Missed It.

BELOW: Jessica Fiorelli and her boyfriend, Russ Reichert, helped clean her mother's home on McFall Road in Apalachin. But Bonnie Fiorelli, Jessica's mother, says that after living through three floods, she has no plans to return to the house. SETH HARRISON / STAFF PHOTO

RIGHT: This sign on the back door of a residence on Front Street in Wellsburg greeted the federal, state and local emergency officials who examined homes there for flood damage. RAY FINGER / STAFF PHOTO

YOU LOOT WE SHOOT

TOP: With food provided by U.S. Foodservice, Southern Baptist Disaster Relief prepared about 20,000 meals for flood victims around Broome County. The meals were distributed by American Red Cross volunteers. Here, SBDR's Creston Schmidt, working at Davis College in Johnson City, carries a tray of chicken patties to be packed for delivery. CASEY STAFF / STAFF PHOTO

BOTTOM: Dorothy Barrett, left, and Conklin Presbyterian Church member Linda Merritt washed the dishes used in cooking the meals distributed to Broome County flood victims. Many volunteers from the church provided aid to flood victims. CASEY STAFF / STAFF PHOTO

ABOVE: Eileen Ahart and others load a vehicle with food, clothing and bedding outside the supply distribution center at the United Methodist church in Candor to go to Owego.

SIMON WHEELER / STAFF PHOTO

TOP: Jen Landry, husband Todd and neighbor Paul Taylor live in a section of Vestal that wasn't affected by the flood. They drove around in a pickup truck, handing out sandwiches, pizza, snacks, drinks and supplies, such as gloves and masks, to those in need. Here, Jen Landry hands a cold drink to Karen Dempsey in the Twin Orchards neighborhood. SETH HARRISON / STAFF PHOTO

BOTTOM LEFT: Kayla Hornberger and April Repetto were part of the American Red Cross disaster relief teams working in flood-affected areas. Here they hand bags containing lunches to Autumn Brown and Carrie Palmieri in the Twin Orchards section of Vestal. SETH HARRISON / STAFF PHOTO

BELOW: Bonnie Emilio is one of a group of friends who got together to make meals for flood victims. They set up a grill on Clinton Street and made deliveries to people in Binghamton and Westover. NANCY DOOLING / STAFF PHOTO

ABOVE: This Vestal Department of Public Works crew was part of the cleanup effort in the Twin Orchards neighborhood. SETH HARRISON / STAFF PHOTO

RIGHT: Dino's Bar and Grill owner Jordan Patch, outside his house on Bradley Avenue in Conklin, pondered his fate while waiting for a FEMA inspector to arrive. The flood damage to his business was so extensive, he said he would not be reopening. CASEY STAFF / STAFF PHOTO

OPPOSITE: Jomaica Johnson, a community relations specialist with FEMA, met with Ron Easton, a resident of the Castle Gardens section of Vestal, to discuss the disaster-relief application process. SETH HARRISON / STAFF PHOTO

LEFT: Volunteers from BonaResponds, a relief organization associated with St. Bonaventure University, demolish ruined walls in Sue Green's home on Maple Street in Athens, Pa. JASON WHONG / STAFF PHOTO

OPPOSITE: BonaResponds volunteer James Torres, 21, dumps ruined insulation onto Sue Green's curb. JASON WHONG / STAFF PHOTO

BELOW: Jake Gallagher knocks out a wall at Las Chicas Tacqueria on Front Street in Owego. JASON WHONG / STAFF PHOTO

ABOVE: Interstate Complete Restoration, Construction & Service employee, Carlos Aguilar, loads a wheelbarrow with scrap metal in the Garden Level of the Binghamton Riverwalk Hotel & Conference Center in downtown Binghamton. The hotel sustained most of its damage on the Garden Level. CASEY STAFF / STAFF PHOTO

2011

For the second time in five years,
flooding has ravaged the communities we live in.

We recovered the first time,
and we will recover again.

Frank E. Berrish
President & CEO
VISIONS Federal Credit Union

I am touched and humbled by the outpouring of support this community has shown. Those who could, gave freely of their time and talents without hesitation to help friends, family, and strangers.

VISIONS, too, suffered damage, though not of the life-altering kind many of our neighbors faced. Several of our local branches were inundated… but we will recover again.

At times like these we really saw the strength of our membership shine. Our members were patient and understanding in light of the challenges that many of them were facing personally. They shared their stories and offered kind words to our employees during the many weeks that followed this devastation. If our members' positive outlook and determination was any reflection of our community as a whole, it is inevitable, that in time, lives will be restored.

Being a part of the credit union community is also a blessing in times like these. We were very fortunate to have support and supplies sent from credit unions in neighboring communities to not only aid in the operational side of our business but also to help many of our employees who suffered personal losses, too. The spirit of the credit union motto "people helping people" shone no brighter than when the State Employees Federal Credit Union donated a mobile office for our use in Owego. It gave our members a sense of normalcy in a time where they needed it most.

There are abundant challenges ahead as this region recovers from this tragedy. Municipalities, businesses, non-profit organizations, neighborhoods, and thousands of people who have called this place home will now wrestle with the complexities and economic realities of a massive rebuilding effort. This will not be an overnight fix.

At VISIONS, our roots are deeply planted in this community, and have been for nearly 50 years. As we always have, we'll be involved in the clean-up and repair, finding innovative ways to offer assistance and support to members and non-members alike.

We will recover again.

Frank E. Berrish

visionsfcu.org

ABOVE: Carol Hawley, a kitchen worker at MacArthur Elementary School in Binghamton, posted a message on the sign in front of the school — a message that says it all.